THE
RADIO

Richard and Louise Spilsbury

Heinemann
LIBRARY

Chicago, Illinois

www.heinemannraintree.com
Visit our website to find out
more information about
Heinemann-Raintree books.

To order:

☎ Phone 888-454-2279

💻 Visit www.heinemannraintree.com
to browse our catalog and order online.

Edited by Louise Galpine and Laura Knowles
Designed by Philippa Jenkins
Original illustrations © Capstone Global Library
    Limited 2012
Picture research by Mica Brancic
Originated by Capstone Global Library Limited
Printed and bound in China by CTPS

15 14 13 12 11
10 9 8 7 6 5 4 3 2 1

Library of Congress Cataloging-in-Publication Data
Spilsbury, Louise.
   The radio / Louise and Richard Spilsbury.
      p. cm.—(Tales of invention)
   Includes bibliographical references and index.
   ISBN 978-1-4329-4878-8 (hc)—ISBN 978-1-4329-
4887-0 (pb) 1. Radio—Juvenile literature. I. Spilsbury,
Richard, 1963- II. Title.
   TK6550.7.S66 2012
   621.384—dc22   2010036495

Acknowledgments
We would like to thank the following for permission
to reproduce photographs: Alamy pp. **4** (© Image
Source/IE040), **17** (© Mary Evans Picture Library), **21**
(© Edward Simons), **22** (© Kuttig - RF – Kids); Corbis
pp. **5** (© Underwood & Underwood), **8** (© Bettmann),
11 (© Bettmann), **12** (© Underwood & Underwood),
15 (© Bettmann), **18** (© Bettmann), **19** (© Sunset
Boulevard), **20** (ClassicStock/© H. Armstrong Roberts),
23 (© Simon Jarratt), **25** (© Douglas Keister), **27**
(Reuters/© STR/Shapi Shacinda); Getty Images
pp. **6** (Science & Society Picture Library), **10** (Hulton
Archive), **24** (Photodisc/StockTrek); The Art Archive
p. **14** (Culver Pictures).

Cover photograph of early-morning workers in a
New York diner, listening to the broadcast of Princess
Elizabeth's wedding in London, England, November 20,
1947, reproduced with permission of Corbis/
© Bettmann.

We would like to thank Walter Podrazik for his
invaluable help in the preparation of this book.

Every effort has been made to contact copyright holders
of material reproduced in this book. Any omissions will
be rectified in subsequent printings if notice is given to
the publisher.

Disclaimer
All the Internet addresses (URLs) given in this book
were valid at the time of going to press. However, due
to the dynamic nature of the Internet, some addresses
may have changed, or sites may have changed or
ceased to exist since publication. While the author
and publisher regret any inconvenience this may cause
readers, no responsibility for any such changes can be
accepted by either the author or the publisher.

CONTENTS

Look for these boxes

Biographies

These boxes tell you about the life of inventors, the dates when they lived, and their important discoveries.

Setbacks

Here we tell you about the experiments that didn't work, the failures, and the accidents.

EUREKA!

These boxes tell you about important events and discoveries, and what inspired them.

Any words appearing in the text in bold, **like this**, are explained in the glossary.

TIMELINE

2011—The timeline shows you when important discoveries and inventions were made.

RADIO TODAY

Millions of people around the world listen to the radio every day. Some listen to up-to-date local or world news. Others exchange opinions on radio call-in shows. Radio entertainment includes music of different styles and live sports commentaries, but radio **broadcasts** can also be important for work and safety. For example, reports can tell sailors when there are rough seas.

Today, radios come in many shapes, sizes, and colors. Have you ever thought about how a radio works?

1837—Samuel Morse invents the telegraph

Before radio, wires strung between poles were the quickest way to send information, such as news, over long distances.

Before radio

The radios we listen to receive signals that carry information through the air. Before radio, messages could only be sent long distances as signals through wires—for example, in early **telegraph** and telephone systems. These were limited by how far the wires extended, and messages could only be carried from one person to another. This meant that news spread much more slowly than today.

The invention of the radio—or "wireless," as it was once known—took many people years to develop and improve. The radio allowed people to listen to the same broadcasts right away and in many places, far from where the signals were sent.

PIONEERS OF RADIO

In the 1860s, Scottish scientist James Clerk Maxwell had the idea that **radio waves** existed. However, it wasn't until 1888 that German physics professor Heinrich Hertz proved this was true. Hertz made sparks of **electricity** jump across a gap between two metal rods, causing pulses of electricity in another machine a short distance away. He proved that electrical energy could be made and **transmitted** through the air in radio waves. If radio waves could carry energy, perhaps they could be used to send information.

Heinrich Hertz was one of the first people to demonstrate radio waves and to imagine the possibilities of radio technology.

Setbacks

Unfortunately, Hertz was not a healthy man. He died at the age of 36, before anyone invented a radio that used his ideas.

What are radio waves?

We cannot see radio waves, but they are **vibrations** carrying energy. There are many different kinds of similar waves moving through air or space. They include microwaves used for cooking food, the light waves in sunlight, and the X-rays we use to see inside bodies.

These waves travel very fast and straight with a regular up-and-down movement, similar to ocean waves. The amount of energy they carry varies by **amplitude** (the height of the wave), **wavelength** (the gap between tips of waves), and **frequency** (the number of waves that go past a certain point each second). Frequency is measured with a unit called a hertz, in honor of Heinrich Hertz.

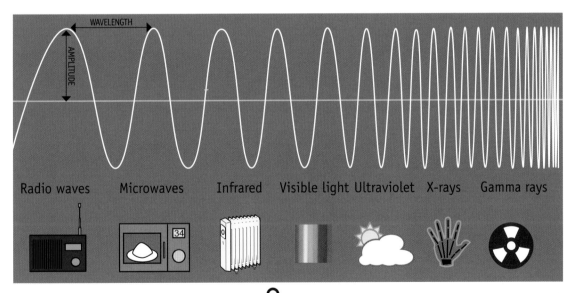

Radio waves · Microwaves · Infrared · Visible light · Ultraviolet · X-rays · Gamma rays

Here you can see all the different types of wave. Waves differ in size and speed. Radio waves have longer wavelengths and lower frequencies than X-rays.

1860s—James Clerk Maxwell has the idea that radio waves exist

1860   1865

Sending waves

Many scientists began to build on Hertz's work to send radio waves further. In 1891 Serbian engineer Nikola Tesla made a **device** that produced and transmitted high-frequency electricity. It was called a Tesla coil. By adding an **antenna** to the coil, Tesla could use the electricity to transmit radio waves to another coil over a distance of 45 kilometers (30 miles). By 1898 Tesla was also using radio waves to control the motor on a model boat!

Early examples of Tesla's coil made large, beautiful sparks of electricity!

Receiving waves

The piece of equipment that sends a radio wave is called a **transmitter**. The part that receives it is a **receiver**. British scientist Oliver Lodge perfected a device he called a "**coherer**." This made receivers better at detecting radio waves.

The coherer was a glass tube with **iron filings** inside. These cohered (clumped) together when radio waves passed through them, then separated again. In 1894 Lodge claimed that he had used his coherer to receive a radio signal around 800 meters (2,625 feet) away from a transmitter.

A transmitter with an antenna can send energy through the air as radio waves to a receiver.

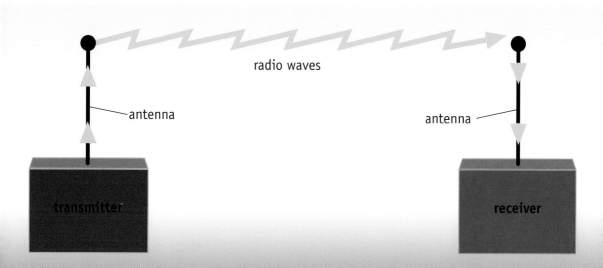

radio waves

antenna

antenna

transmitter

receiver

9

THE FIRST RADIO?

Italian scientist Guglielmo Marconi realized that to send signals across very long distances, you need a very high **antenna**. This meant the signals could travel in straight lines without being blocked by buildings, hills, or other objects. In 1899 Marconi sent **radio waves** across the English Channel. Then, in 1901, he became the first person to send a **transatlantic** message using **Morse Code**. He sent it from Cornwall, England, to Newfoundland, Canada. Marconi was the first person to show the world how practical radio could be used for communication.

EUREKA!

In 1901 Marconi tried to use a balloon to hold an antenna high in the air. But when winds blew it away, he used a kite about 70 meters (230 feet) high in the sky to send the first transatlantic **broadcast**.

Marconi and his team relied on kites to make the first radio broadcast possible.

1888—Heinrich Hertz proves electrical energy can be transmitted in radio waves (see page 6)

The power of patents

Marconi held the first valid **patent** for radio. A patent is official proof that someone has invented something new, so that other people cannot copy it without permission. In fact, many people claimed to have invented radio first, but they did not bother to get patents or other proof! These people included Russian Alexander Popov, who **transmitted** and received radio waves in 1895, and Indian J. C. Bose, who transmitted signals over 1.6 kilometers (1 mile) in 1896. Other people claim that pioneers Tesla and Lodge were really the inventors of radio, because their ideas were used by Marconi.

This is Marconi's first radio. Was Marconi the real "father of radio," or just a better businessman than the other inventors?

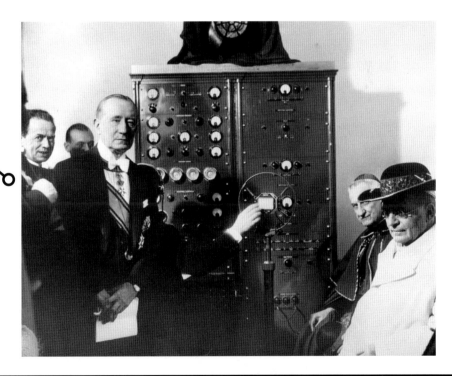

1891—Nikola Tesla makes a **device** to produce and transmit high-**frequency electricity** (see page 8)

1894—Oliver Lodge makes a **coherer** to receive a radio signal 800 meters (2,625 feet) away (see page 9)

1895—Alexander Popov transmits and receives radio waves in Russia

1890

1895

1895— Marconi sends radio waves across a room

1896—Indian scientist J. C. Bose transmits radio signals over 1.6 kilometers (1 mile) (see page 11)

1898— Tesla builds a radio-controlled model boat (see page 8)

1899— Marconi sends radio waves across the English Channel

1900—Reginald Fessenden sends the first voice signals by radio over a short distance (see page 16)

1895

1900

Guglielmo Marconi (1874-1937)

Guglielmo Marconi became interested in **electricity** as a schoolchild. Later, he turned two rooms in his family's home in Italy into laboratories where he carried out experiments. It is believed that in 1895 Marconi managed to send radio waves from a **transmitter** at one end of a room to a **receiver** that then rang a bell at the other end. He soon adapted this **device** to send messages in Morse code.

When the Italian government showed no interest in his invention, Marconi and his mother moved to England and set up their own company. This company applied for patents across the world and organized events to get publicity. For example, in 1898 they installed a radio on the yacht of Britain's Queen Victoria, so she could send messages from land to her son on board. By the early 1900s, Marconi's radio invention was being used in many places around the world. For his achievements, Marconi was awarded the 1909 Nobel Prize for Physics.

During World War I (1914–18), Marconi returned to Italy, where he was in charge of wireless **telegraph** communication for the army. Then in 1931, to celebrate the 30th anniversary of his first transatlantic message, he spoke in a radio broadcast. When he died in 1937, radio stations around the world stopped transmitting for a short period of silence during his funeral.

13

1901—Marconi sends the first transatlantic radio message (see page 10)

1906—Fessenden sends voice signals several hundred miles (see page 16)

1909—Marconi is awarded the Nobel Prize for Physics

1905

1910

Using early radios

The first radios could only send messages by Morse Code. They were mostly used for communication between ships and land, because places on land continued to use wired telegraph systems. Using Morse Code, ships could receive news and weather reports and call for help if they needed it.

In written Morse Code, letters of the alphabet are shown as dots and dashes. To send the code by radio, transmitters are switched on and off to make short and long signals. For example, the distress signal SOS (...---...) was sent as three short, three long, and three short pulses by radio.

In the early 1900s, all new ships had radios for safety. Skilled radio operators were essential on land and at sea.

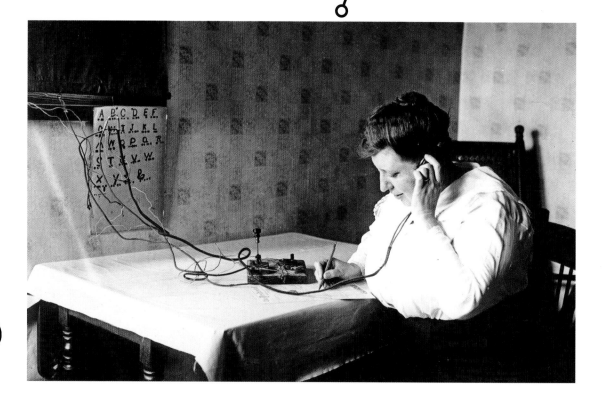

1910—Murderer Dr. Crippen is caught because of radio

1912—Radio distress calls from the *Titanic* save 700 people's lives

1910

1915

The tragedy of the *Titanic* proved to the world the importance of radios for safety on ships.

Radio rescue

In 1912 the luxury ocean liner *Titanic* was on its first voyage when it hit an iceberg and began to sink. There were 2,200 passengers and crew on board. The two Marconi company radio operators on board sent distress calls in Morse Code to nearby ships. Their use of radio allowed 700 people to be rescued.

EUREKA!

In 1910 Dr. Hawley Harvey Crippen murdered his wife and fled London with his girlfriend, on a ship bound for Canada. The captain became suspicious of Crippen's behavior because the girlfriend was disguised as a boy. He used the ship's radio to inform the police, who had discovered Crippen's wife's body. The police got on a faster ship and arrested Crippen for the crime before he could escape to Canada.

WIRELESS WORLD

The next big invention after sending **Morse Code** signals was to **broadcast** the human voice. Canadian engineer Reginald Fessenden first did this in 1900, but his voice only traveled a few feet. Fessenden set up a powerful **transmitter**, with a microphone connected, that produced a steady radio signal from an **antenna**. The changing pattern of electrical signals made by the microphone as he spoke into it caused the **radio waves** to increase. Radio **receivers** have **loudspeakers** that convert radio wave signals back into sound.

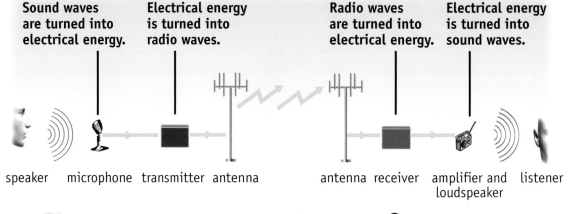

| Sound waves are turned into electrical energy. | Electrical energy is turned into radio waves. | Radio waves are turned into electrical energy. | Electrical energy is turned into sound waves. |

speaker   microphone   transmitter   antenna   antenna   receiver   amplifier and   listener
                                                                                  loudspeaker

EUREKA!

The first known radio broadcast was on Christmas Eve 1906, when Reginald Fessenden **transmitted** readings from the Bible and music he played on his violin. Ships' radio operators heard his voice up to several hundred miles away.

This diagram shows how sound can be transmitted through radio waves.

Radios at war

During World War I (1914–18), all work on radio development focused on its use in battle. In the United Kingdom, the government took control of the Marconi Company and began training new operators. All armies and navies in the war used radio to pass on orders and communications. Radio could also be used to locate enemy transmitters in order to plan attacks.

Public broadcasts

After the war, more people had heard about and wanted to use this amazing new technology. In 1920 Marconi started broadcasting music to the public. The first radio broadcasting station aimed at the general public opened in the United States in the same year. Other stations soon followed, at first mostly broadcasting talk and music.

Here, German soldiers are using a mobile radio station during World War I.

1937—The first radio telescope is made (see page 24)

The Radio Age

The 1920s and 1930s were a boom time for radio. People rushed to buy new radios with built-in speakers that the whole family could listen to together. Hundreds of radio stations broadcast on different **frequencies**. People turned the dials on their receivers to find particular frequencies, or they kept turning until they heard something of interest.

In the United States, between 1923 and 1930, 60 percent of families bought radio receivers!

1940—Hedy Lamarr invents a way to fool enemy radio-tracking systems

In November 1925, a radio station in Nashville, Tennessee, started to broadcast a show called *Grand Ole Opry*. The show featured performances of country music in front of live audiences. By the 1930s, it was so popular it had to move to a larger studio. Today, *Grand Ole Opry* is the longest-running radio show in history.

Hedy Lamarr invented a way to stop the Nazis in World War II from receiving radio broadcasts to the U.S. troops.

World War II

During World War II (1939–45), radio became an important tool for people to hear war news, warnings of attacks, and **propaganda** from their leaders. Throughout Germany, loudspeakers put up in streets broadcast messages from the Nazi leader Adolf Hitler. Radio was also used by armed forces to defend against the enemy. Signals from radios could be used to detect an enemy's hiding place.

In the 1940s, radio signals used to control U.S. torpedoes were being tracked and jammed by Nazis. U.S. movie star Hedy Lamarr realized the signals would be impossible to jam if transmitters and receivers rapidly switched frequencies. Only operators who knew the sequence of frequencies could unjumble the messages. Lamarr's "frequency hopping" idea was ignored at first, but it was eventually used by the U.S. Army in the 1960s—and recently in cell phones!

19

1954—The first **transistor** radio goes on sale (see pages 20 and 21)

1950   1955

Portable radios

Early radios had large **valves**. These were special glass tubes that **amplified** sound signals so sound could be heard through a loudspeaker. This meant that early radios were big and bulky. In 1948 the **transistor** was invented independently by two German scientists, Herbert Mataré and Heinrich Welker. Transistors did the same job as the valves, but they were much smaller.

Radio programming

As radios became common in U.S. homes, different types of entertainment—such as soap operas, Westerns, and variety shows—became popular. But after World War II, more people started to buy televisions, and television took over as the major source for these kinds of entertainment. In response, most radio stations focused once again on music, news, sports, or call-in talk shows.

Small transistor radios were powered with small batteries so they could be carried around and listened to anywhere.

Digital radio

Digital radio was developed in the 1990s by a group of European radio broadcasters and manufacturers. With this system, a transmitter sends fragments of signals as a code made up of numbers. The receiver pieces together the codes into a complete signal. There are several advantages over earlier radio signals. Digital signals have less **interference** (crackling sounds). In addition to sound, text and images can also be packed into the same frequencies.

Few people could afford the first transistor radios when they went on sale in the United States in 1954. They cost the equivalent of $400 today!

A digital radio collects coded radio signals from the air and combines them, in order to form uninterrupted sounds.

We use **radio waves** and signals for listening to music and voices, but also to control many things, from toy robots, cars, and boats to cell phones and televisions.

How radio control works

How can you use radio waves to control the movement of a toy car? When you press a trigger on a handset, the **transmitter** sends a sequence of electrical pulses as radio waves. The toy car has a **receiver** that searches for signals on that **frequency**. Electronics inside the car decode the pulses to make motors work to move the car. For example, 16 pulses might make a toy car move forward, while 40 pulses move it into reverse.

Radio waves can be used to have fun as well as for communication.

EUREKA!

The name "Bluetooth" comes from a Danish Viking king named Bluetooth, who lived in the 900s. King Bluetooth united fighting tribes, and the Bluetooth radio link was created to "unite" lots of different devices!

Bluetooth

In 1998 Ericsson, a Swedish manufacturer of cell phones, formed a group of electronics companies to produce **devices** that worked using Bluetooth technology. Bluetooth is a special radio link that allows laptop computers, cell phones, and other fixed and portable devices to transfer data over short distances without being connected by wires.

Bluetooth sends sounds and information by radio waves. It changes frequency thousands of times a second to avoid radio **interference**.

People often use Bluetooth headsets to speak on cell phones.

Radio telescopes

Radio waves are also used to detect distant objects in space. Stars, galaxies, and other objects in space naturally give off radio waves. But they are so far away that these signals are very weak when they reach Earth. Radio engineer Grote Reber made the first radio telescope to capture such signals in 1937. Today, radio telescopes have a giant **antenna** to pick up the radio waves, a receiver to **amplify** the signals, and a computer to interpret them.

Some people hope giant dish-shaped antennae on radio telescopes might capture communications from life on distant planets!

In 1931 U.S. radio engineer Karl Jansky could not figure out why his radio was crackling. When he pointed the antenna to the sky, he realized that radio waves from distant stars were creating interference.

1990s—People are able to use Global Positioning Systems (GPS) to locate positions on Earth

1990s—Digital radio is invented

1991—The wind-up radio is invented (see page 27)

Radio navigation

The same types of antennae used in radio telescopes are also used to track and collect data from **satellites** in space. In **Global Positioning Systems (GPS)**, radio signals are sent from a network of satellites in space to receivers on the ground. The receivers collect and convert the signals, to tell people where they are or where they want to go. The first GPS satellites were meant for army and navy use, but by 1993 GPS was being used by ordinary people, too.

In cars, satellite navigation systems use GPS to show drivers which route to take.

1994—The first Internet radio station is **broadcast** (see page 26)

1998—Bluetooth wireless communication is invented (see page 23)

Today, radio sets are very different from the early models. They come in many sizes and shapes, can be set into sunglasses or watches, and have access to thousands of programs. What will radio be like in the future?

Changing broadcasts

In the future, there may not even be separate radio sets anymore, as more stations **broadcast** over the Internet to wireless **devices** such as cell phones or laptops. In 1994 a U.S. radio station called WXYC became the first to broadcast on the Internet. In 2008 Sirius XM formed the largest **satellite** radio service in the world. People pay a monthly fee for a **receiver** and access to radio broadcasts. It has a very high-quality sound and no **interference**.

EUREKA!

In 1991 Trevor Baylis watched a TV program about the spread of **AIDS** in Africa. It described how difficult it was to tell people how to avoid the disease, because people could not afford or did not have electricity to use power radios. Baylis went to his workshop and made the first wind-up radio, using spare parts he found there.

Wind-up radios make their own power. This one is being used to broadcast classes to children in Zambia who cannot afford to go to school.

Green technology

Making **electricity** to run radios and other machines causes problems like **pollution** and **global warming**. So, people have invented radios that run on other sources of power, such as solar power (energy from the Sun), and wind-up radios. These radios are also useful in places where electricity is unavailable, such as after a natural disaster like an earthquake, or in remote parts of the world.

2008—Sirius XM satellite radio service begins to broadcast

TIMELINE

1837
Samuel Morse invents the **telegraph**

1860s
James Clerk Maxwell has the idea that **radio waves** exist

1888
Heinrich Hertz proves electrical energy can be **transmitted** in radio waves

1906
Fessenden sends voice signals several hundred miles

1901
Marconi sends the first **transatlantic** radio message

1900
Reginald Fessenden sends the first voice signals by radio over a short distance

1909
Marconi is awarded the Nobel Prize for Physics

1912
Radio distress calls from the *Titanic* save 700 people's lives

1920
The first public radio **broadcasting** station is opened in the United States

2008
Sirius XM **satellite** radio service begins to broadcast

1998
Bluetooth wireless communication is invented

1994
The first Internet radio station is broadcast

1891
Nikola Tesla makes a **device** to produce and transmit high-**frequency electricity**

1894
Oliver Lodge makes a **coherer** to receive a radio signal 800 meters (2,625 feet) away

1895
Alexander Popov transmits and receives radio waves in Russia. Guglielmo Marconi sends radio waves across a room.

1899
Marconi sends radio waves across the English Channel

1898
Tesla builds a radio-controlled model boat

1896
Indian scientist J. C. Bose transmits radio signals over 1.6 kilometers (1 mile)

1930s
Different forms of entertainment, such as soap operas and Westerns, become popular forms of radio programming

1937
The first radio telescope is made

1940
Hedy Lamarr invents a way to fool enemy radio-tracking systems

1991
The wind-up radio is invented

1990s
Digital radio is invented. People are able to use **GPS** to locate positions on Earth.

1954
The first **transistor** radio goes on sale

GLOSSARY

AIDS stands for "acquired immunodeficiency syndrome," a disease for which there is no known cure. It is most common in African countries.

amplify increase volume of a sound signal

amplitude height of a wave and also a measure of its strength

antenna (plural: antennae) device converting radio signals into electricity, and electricity into radio signals

broadcast sending out radio signals from a transmitter for anyone to receive

coherer early device to detect radio signals

device piece of equipment wth a particular purpose

electricity form of energy from the flow of an electric charge

frequency measure of the number of times something, such as a wave peak, passes a point in a given time

Global Positioning System (GPS) instrument that finds a precise position on Earth using radio time signals from satellites

global warming gradual warming of Earth's atmosphere caused mainly by gases released when we burn certain fuels

interference when obstacles or other radio waves interrupt a radio signal, often causing a crackling sound

iron filings tiny pieces of iron

loudspeaker machine that converts electrical signals into sound waves

Morse Code system of dots and dashes that stand for letters, numbers, and other symbols

patent official proof that an invention, idea, or process was the idea of a particular person, and protection from it being copied

pollution when air, soil, or water is made dirty with harmful substances

propaganda specific ideas or views spread around to influence others. For example, Adolf Hitler's propaganda encouraged people to join the Nazi Party.

radio wave type of wave used for broadcasting radio signals

receiver device that receives radio signals using an antenna and converts them into sound

satellite human-made object put into space to move around Earth, often to transmit radio and other signals

telegraph system for sending messages by radio waves or electric wires

transatlantic across the Atlantic Ocean

transistor device to amplify an electrical signal that can switch on and off

transmit send signals containing information

transmitter device that converts electrical signals into radio waves and sends out the signals

valve early device that acts like a transistor

vibration move rapidly up and down or back and forth

wavelength distance between the peaks of one wave and the next

FIND OUT MORE

Books

Fedunkiw, Marianne. *Inventing the Radio* (*Breakthrough Inventions*). New York: Crabtree, 2007.

Malam, John. *Guglielmo Marconi* (*Great Scientists*). Chicago: Raintree, 2009.

O'Shei, Tim. *Marconi and Tesla: Pioneers of Radio Communication* (*Inventors Who Changed the World*). Berkeley Heights, N.J.: MyReportLinks.com Books, 2008.

Websites

www.fcc.gov/cgb/kidszone/faqs_radio.html
This website of the U.S. Federal Communications Commission answers some common questions about how radios work.

www.nrao.edu/index.php/learn/radioastronomy/radiocommunication
Go to this National Radio Astronomy Observatory website to find out more about sound and radio waves.

http://boyslife.org/games/online-games/575/morse-code-machine/
Visit this website to try Morse Code.

Places to visit

The Museum of Broadcast Communications
676 North LaSalle Drive
Suite 424
Chicago, Illinois 60654
www.museum.tv

The Radio and Television Museum
2608 Mitchellville Road
Bowie, Maryland 20716
www.radiohistory.org

INDEX